Knowing the Notes

for viola

by Cassia Harvey
edited by Judith Harvey

CHP133
ISBN 978-1-932823-32-5

6403 N. 6th Street
Philadelphia, PA 19126
www.charveypublications.com

Knowing the Notes for Viola

The Note D; open string

Cassia Harvey

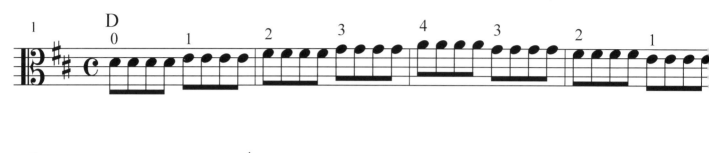

Yankee Doodle

Traditional/arr. C. Harvey

ow many D notes are in this song?

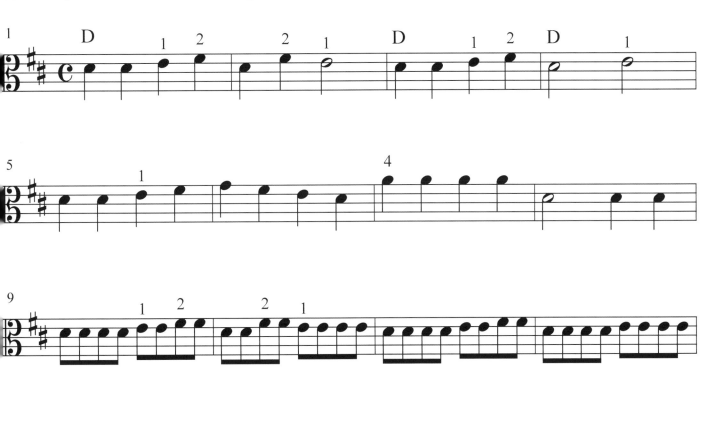

The Note E

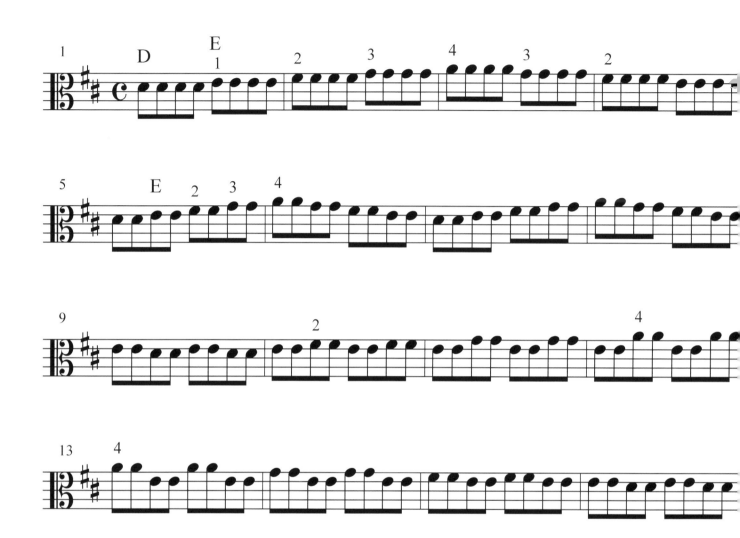

The New World and Variation

Dvorak/arr. C. Harvey

ow many E notes are in this song?

ow many beats are in a measure?

The Note F♯

Dance with Variation

Praetorious/arr. C. Harvey

ow many F♯ notes are in this song?

The Note G

German Dance

Traditional/arr. C. Harvey

ow many G notes are in this song?

The Note A; 4th finger

Allegretto

ow many A notes are in this song?

Campagnoli/arr. C. Harvey

ow many beats are in a measure?

The Note F♮

Farandole

Bizet/arr. C. Harvey

ow many F notes are in this song?

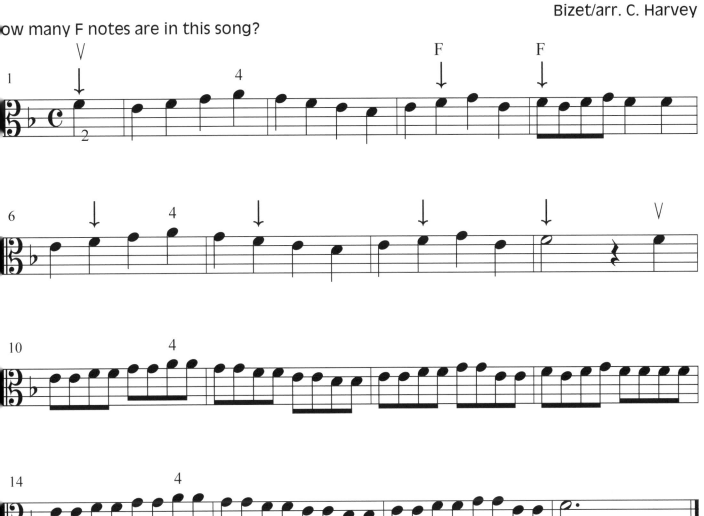

The Note A; open string

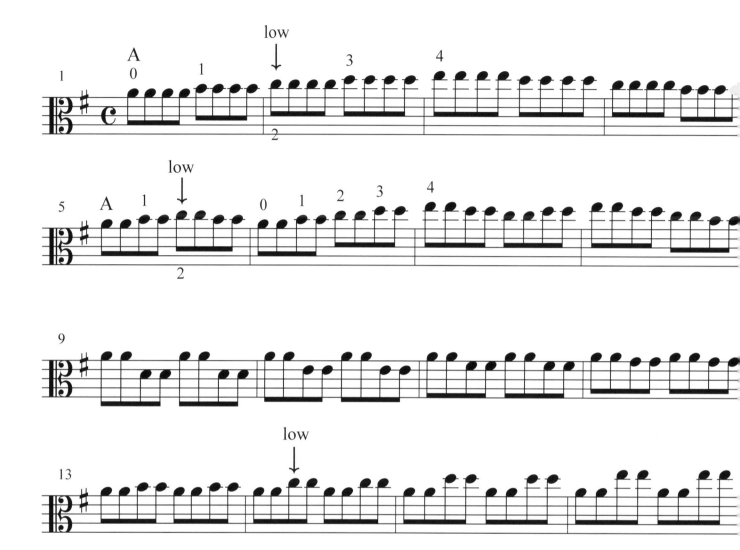

The Prince of Denmark's March

Clarke/arr. C. Harvey

The Note B

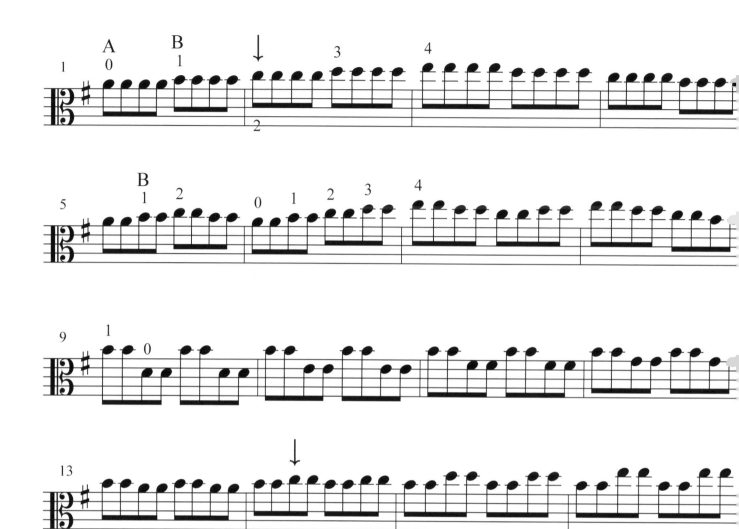

Lavender's Blue

Traditional/arr. C. Harvey

The Note C

Greenland Fisheries

Traditional/arr. C. Harvey

The Note D

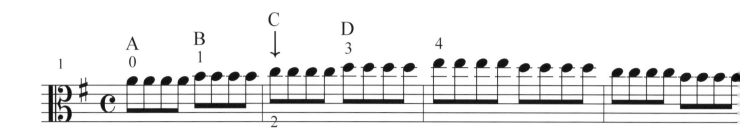

Soldier, Will You Marry Me?

Traditional/arr. C. Harvey

The Note E

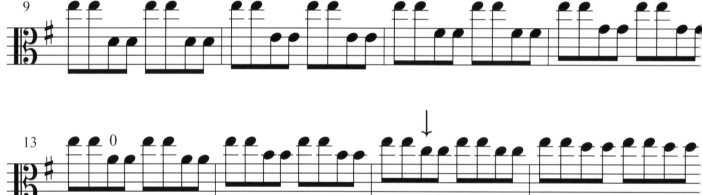

Turkey in the Straw Variation

Traditional/arr. C. Harvey

The Note D on the G string

Cassia Harve

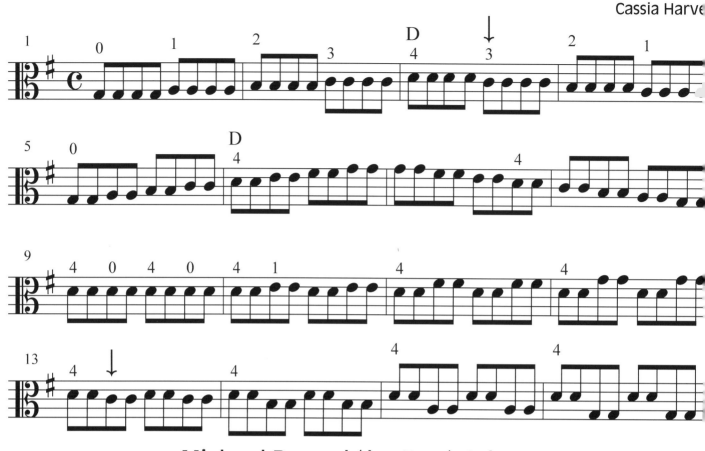

Michael Rowed the Boat Ashore

Traditional/arr. C. Harve

The Note C on the G string

Cassia Harvey

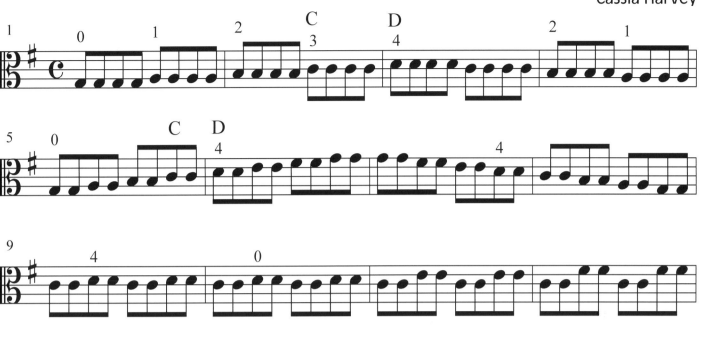

Drill, Ye Tarriers, Drill

Traditional/arr. C. Harvey

The Note B on the G string

Cassia Harve

Goober Peas

Traditional/arr. C. Harve

The Note A on the G string

Cassia Harvey

Little Dance

Turk/arr. C. Harvey

The Note G; open string

Cassia Harve

My Old Wagon

Traditional/arr. C. Harve

The Note B♭ on the G string

Cassia Harvey

The Caissons go Rolling Along

Traditional/arr. C. Harvey

The Note G on the C string

Cassia Harve

Rigaudon

Rameau/arr. C. Harve

The Note F♯ on the C string

Cassia Harvey

Polly Wolly Doodle

Traditional/arr. C. Harvey

The Note E on the C string

Cassia Harve

March

Bach/arr. C. Harve

The Note D on the C string

Cassia Harvey

Allegro

Rameau/arr. C. Harvey

The Note C; open string

Cassia Harve

The China Figurine

Rebikov/arr. C. Harve

1

Third Position for the Viola, Book One

Cassia Harvey

First Shifting on the D string

First Shifting on the A string

Made in the USA
Middletown, DE
18 January 2020